Made to Sparkle

How to Shine in Your Studies
and Lead Well in School

Yvette Lanier

Made to Sparkle: How to Shine in Your Studies and Lead Well in School
ISBN: 978-0-578-88490-5
Copyright © 2021 by Yvette Lanier

Printed by Ingram Sparks in the United States of America.

Dedication

To my nieces—Francesca, Naiana, Dez'Siree, Dasia, and Yvette—and every young girl who desires to pursue a good path and shine for Christ: You are my daily inspiration to continue to pursue the path of a virtuous woman. My hope is that you will know the truth: you too can sparkle!

"A capable, intelligent, and virtuous woman
who is he who can find her? She is far more
precious than jewels and her value is far
above rubies or pearls."

—PROVERBS 31:10 (AMPC)

Contents

My Personal Letter to You   7

Chapter 1 (Charlotte's Story): Sparkle With Faith

You have an Invitation to Shine   *11*

Chapter 2 (Grace's Story): Sparkle With Leadership

I Believe in You   *25*

Chapter 3 (Violet's Story): Sparkle With Courage

You Are Gifted   *43*

Chapter 4 (Olivia's Story): Sparkle With Confidence

God Sees Something in You   *57*

Chapter 5 (Jasmine's Story): Sparkle With Clear Vision

You Hold the Power of Focus   *65*

Epilogue: Need to Talk?

The Story Behind the Story   *81*

Dear Amazing Girl,

I am so glad you picked up this book. Did you know there is a time and season for everything? It is your season to shine in school and lead well! Within your heart are gifts and talents God has given you. He made you fearfully and wonderfully. By using these gifts, whatever you achieve brings glory to Him!

I was once where you are, but I had no one leading me with godly character or showing me what it meant to be a virtuous young lady. No one in my immediate family went to church or studied the Bible. It was not until I graduated from Bible college that I stumbled upon Proverbs 31:10–31. The opening line captured my heart, *"A capable, intelligent, and virtuous woman—who is he who can find her?"* (Proverbs 31:10 AMPC). I wanted to be her. I prayed to God, "Help me become her."

Every day, I continue to see how capable and intelligent I am, as I pursue righteousness.

But I also want to help other young girls see that they can "be her" too.

You can develop godly character in school and shine bright!

It would have been wonderful for me to have this foundation while I was in high school because it would have saved me from so many mistakes. I struggled with insecurity. I never told myself I was beautiful or smart. Today I am very thankful for God's Word because it reminds me of who I am.

I am also thankful for God's grace because it continues to give me opportunities to share His amazing love with others. One way I joyfully share compassion is by helping women find hope after facing an unplanned pregnancy. Many find themselves afraid, confused, and alone. It is an honor to remind them that God is ready to help them on this new journey and help them know that they are not alone.

You are not alone, either! Every young woman can accomplish great things regardless of what has happened in the past or what challenges are on the horizon. As you read these pages, I pray that you will begin to see who you are and what you can accomplish as you develop your character in Christ.

A good heart sends forth shimmers of His light and glory that will inspire others. ***And I know this: your heart is made to sparkle!***

Yours truly,

Yvette Lanier

CHAPTER ONE

Charlotte's Story
Sparkle With Faith

Norah prayed out loud, "Dear God, you're really big. Charlotte says that you're good too. I'm pretty sure you like to have fun because you made the rainbow. Can you help us have a cool dance? It is called *A Night to Remember* because honestly, sometimes . . . well . . ." Her voice trailed off for a moment as she searched for words. "We feel forgotten, and it really hurts. But we know that you remember our names. Thank you, God."

Charlotte's eyes welled with tears. Norah was an 11-year-old who lived in an orphanage since she was five. She was rescued from an abandoned drug house and brought to Hope for Children. She never had a visitor in six years. Yet despite her hardships, Norah always held on to hope. Her childlike faith inspired Charlotte.

When both said, "Amen in Jesus' Name," Charlotte's heart was still heavy. The deadline for the dance was just one week away, and she was still short $1,500 on the budget for food, decorations, and dresses for the girls. She didn't want to break her promise of a fabulous event!

Maybe it was a lofty goal for a senior in high school. Charlotte was a star student, but she started to doubt herself.

She attended Grove Private School in Greenwood and spent Wednesday mornings volunteering at the orphanage before her financial class. This was a privilege given to honor roll students. She was moved with compassion for these young girls, and knew that God reminded His people to care for the orphans.

Charlotte had a few short days to make the dream a reality—*A Night to Remember*, the dance for 13 middle school girls who never got a phone call or a hug. For one fabulous night, she wanted them to forget they were orphans and feel overwhelming love. She couldn't disappoint the girls. It *had* to happen! Everyone she asked donated to the cause—her parents, the principal, her youth pastor, and even the orphanage itself, but she was still short of the goal.

There was still one more person to ask—the last one on Charlotte's list. She dreaded it because Ava Hamilton never gave to anyone, not even her own brother when he raised money for his Boy Scout trip! She said he needed to learn how to do it on his own. Ava never even gave homeless people money to get food. The needs didn't matter; she always said no.

Avas's family owned the largest accounting firm in the city, and she was brilliant in her business too. She was the president of the Grove's young entrepreneur program. She and her sister made the front page of the business section of the local newspaper—named among ten young entrepreneurs on the horizon. She had dreams of running her father's business and becoming CEO.

On Wednesday, Charlotte glanced at the clock as she finished some volunteer tasks at the orphanage. *Oh dear! I need to get to class in 20 minutes!* She tossed the last of the plates in the dishwasher and dashed for door. She loved her personal finance class, and today she would see

Ava. They were great friends, and Charlotte respected her for striving toward her dreams. She was always inspired to do the same.

The bell rang for the second-hour class to begin, and Mr. Smith told everyone to gather in their groups. Ava and Charlotte were grouped with three other classmates for the team project. Their assignment was to practice running a bank.

As they worked on their budget, Ava blurted out, "I have some great news! My dad is letting me invest in the stock market since I'll be turning 18 in two weeks."

Charlotte gave her a high-five and replied, "That's great! Hasn't that been a dream of yours since freshman year? You're making it happen, girl!"

"My dad's stocks are doing great too," Ava added. "We're looking at purchasing a new boat for our lake house for the summer and planning a trip to visit my uncle in London."

Even though it was different from her family, Charlotte was proud of Ava and her family's success. Her accomplishments were inspiring. It's probably why they were good friends. Ava always made her aim higher and be better.

Charlotte mustered the courage to ask the big question. "Hey Ava, do you know the orphanage where I volunteer every Wednesday before our class?"

"Yes, your school project."

"Well, we're hosting *A Night to Remember* for the girls and need $1,500 to reach our goal. I understand you don't usually give to organizations, but would you give one time to the girls at Hope?"

Ava thought about it and said, "No, we never give, Charlotte, not to any cause. My family is focused on growing and expanding the accounting business. I can't deviate from that. I'm sure you understand, right?"

Charlotte nodded, but her heart sank. She hoped this would be the answer to Norah's prayer. Now she needed a miracle. She thought of the list of people she knew and silently prayed, *God, I have no one else to ask. Please help!* Even though she prayed, she couldn't see how it could happen. Charlotte mentally prepared how to tell the girls their dance would not happen.

"Will you be attending youth game night at church tonight?" Ava's question interrupted Charlotte's thoughts.

"Of course, and I'm inviting one of the girl's from the Orphanage." Inwardly Charlotte thought, *I need an event take my mind off the project. I could use a little more prayer and faith too.* She remembered a verse the youth pastor spoke about the week before: *"So then faith comes by hearing, and hearing by the word of God"* (Rom. 10:17 NKJV). She promised to read her Bible and build her faith before game night started. *Thanks for the reminder, God!*

That night Norah spotted Ava standing near the snack bar chatting with friends and ran towards her smiling, "Is your name Ava?"

"Yes," said Ava and returned Norah's smile.

"Hi, I'm Norah, Charlotte's friend. Charlotte told me all about you. You're her best friend, and she's said a lot of great things about you. Can you be my best friend too?"

Ava was taken back by her question. She never had a friend so much younger than her, but she was delighted Norah asked and said an enthusiastic, "Sure!"

Norah grinned., "Would you like to play four-square? Charlotte said you're really good at it."

"Why not? Let's go for it."

The youth pastor, Jake, saw the scene unfold. He and his wife walked up to Charlotte. "Do you think Norah can soften Ava's heart?"

Charlotte phone her youth pastors after Ava said no and asked for encouragement and wisdom about how not to let the girls down. "I'm not sure," she replied with hesitancy.

Jake nudged her shoulder and said with a wink, "Have a little faith! Remember?"

Charlotte nodded and her worried expression melted as she watched Ava and Norah laugh and play, bouncing the ball and hitting it around the four squares.

When the youth pastor called everyone into the auditorium for a brief message, Norah, Charlotte, and Ava found seats with the others. He taught about refreshing others through kindness, friendliness, encouragement, and generosity. "When we give to those in need, God blesses us in return." He prayed and ended the message with a worship song.

With the notes still hanging in the air, Ava leaned over and whispered to Charlotte, "Is Norah one of the orphan girls who will be a part of the project?"

"Yes, she is—and 12 more girls."

"Norah is so sweet and fun," Ava replied. "I'm going to ask my dad to help with *A Night to Remember*." She noticed Charlotte's raised eyebrows and said, "Norah deserves it! Besides . . . I'm beginning to see what Pastor Jake is talking about, that it's good to give to those in need."

"Wow! Thanks, Ava! You have no idea how much this means to the girls and to me." Charlotte hugged her and thanked God in her heart for His miracle.

How Can You Sparkle With Faith?

You Have an Invitation to Shine

Many things in this world can hold our hearts. It may be friendships, popularity, money, fashion, television, sports, or a social media status. For Ava, it was success and wealth. None of these things are bad within themselves, but the big question is: Does it draw our hearts away from fully trusting God and His amazing plans? Sometimes we have to look within and see what's holding our hearts from complete surrender.

Can I ask a real question? As a young woman, what is holding the most important place in your heart? In order to sparkle, there must be willingness to do a "heart check." Are you seeking anything more than God? Are you willing to give up things in your life to walk in God's good ways?

I know it can be tough to examine your heart, but what if I told you that no matter how big you can think and dream, God has more for you? He has such great plans for you—plans for you to thrive in your school and have greater influence in your daily life, plans to be a wonderful and joyful blessing to those around you, and plans to bless you too.

Letting other areas go is a choice everyone has to make—sometimes daily. May I encourage you? Go for it! Jesus said, *"What is impossible with man is possible with God"* (Luke 18:27 NIV). It may seem hard, but it is not an impossible choice to make God is by your side to help you every step of the way!

Choose to take a good path. Jesus said the way that leads to destruction is broad, but the path that leads to life is narrow (Matt. 7:13–14). You can be courageous and take a less-traveled road by saying "Yes!" to God and putting Him first.

I invite you to take the step! If you haven't already, make the commitment to give your heart completely to Jesus. He is waiting for you with open arms—arms wide open to receive you just as you are in this moment. Maybe you feel like your heart has become cold, and far from God. Draw near to Him again! If your heart is tugging at you and pounding in you right now—or if you just know you need to take the next step—pray the following prayer out loud:

> *"God, you said that if I call upon the name of the Lord, I shall be saved. Today, I confess Jesus as my Lord and Savior. I repent of my sins and turn away from things that are less than Your best. Help me to walk in Your good ways and follow after You. Thank you for loving me, leading me in the way of life, and making my heart new so I can sparkle."*

If you prayed that prayer, you accepted an extraordinary invitation to an adventure with God. I am praying for you and asking God to show you His awesome plan for your life. Be sure to read the Bible! Start by reading a Psalm a day or look up the references you see in this book. If you have a smartphone, read them in different versions of the Bible. God's Word will show you who you are and give you a heart to do His will—a heart full of goodness, love, peace, and kindness. In His eyes, you are smart, capable, and beautiful! You are made to shine bright!

Lastly, I encourage you to share this wonderful news with someone. Saying this prayer is a big deal, and God wants you to share your story with others. You can do it, girl!

Sparkle & Shine

Reflect on what you've read!

Write a Prayer: God loves it when we draw near to Him. *"Come close to God, and God will come close to you"* (James 4:8 NLT). Write a prayer to God asking Him to help you give your heart fully to Him, His goodness, and His ways. Even if you're afraid or unsure, His promises are still good today to strengthen you when you feel weak (2 Cor. 2:19).

_____

_____

_____

_____

_____

_____

_____

_____

_____

_____

" For I know the plans I have for you,' says the Lord. They are plans for good and not for disaster, to give you a future and a hope."

—JEREMIAH 29:11 (NLT)

CHAPTER TWO

Grace's Story

Sparkle With Leadership

Coach Tillman looked at up at the rafters and took a deep breath before addressing the volleyball team. Her whistle hung around her neck, like it always did, but her black hair seemed to weigh down her slouched shoulders. Concern clouded her face as she searched for hope in the girls' eyes.

"The last time Fields High School won the state championship was in 1994. This year, many of you are out of shape, uninterested, or just playing because of your parents expect you to." A look of worry flickered across her face. "If we don't win this year, they're going to cut the program and put the funds elsewhere."

She turned to a young freshman and said, "We need you Grace. You have the talent and passion to lead this team. Are you up for the challenge?"

Grace's eyes grew large and her mouth began to open. Nothing came out. She just blinked and wondered, *Did she just ask me to be the captain of the Varsity team?* Grace's eyes grew large and her mouth began to open, but nothing came out. She just blinked.

Coach Tillman laughed and answered as if she read her mind, "Yes, Grace, I am asking you if you are willing to be the captain."

Grace looked around the locker room before answering. Some eyes glared, others were dull, but she didn't see anyone with a glint of desire. That was her cue. "Yes, coach. If you need me, I'll do my best!"

It was no secret that Grace had talent. She auditioned for the JV team along with her classmates but was added to the varsity roster without a tryout. Her resume was as impressive as her love of the game. She played volleyball since age six, when she joined a recreational league. Her parents watched her skill develop and invested in training clinics. She helped her middle school team win three championships, but winning came with a price: practicing all summer.

Even when Grace was exhausted by the extra workouts, her dad spurred her on. "C'mon, Gracie! You know that practice only makes you better and stronger!" His encouraging voice and proud smile fueled her competitive spirit. Together they built her confidence, and it showed.

It also helped that she was 5'8" and often one the of the tallest girls on the court. Her dad made sure they practiced for hours in the summer, even when she felt exhausted.

He reminded, "practice only makes you better and stronger."

She was right. she was better and stronger, but was she a leader?

As the team made their way out to the court for practice, Coach Tillman draped her arm around Grace with the first smile anyone saw that day, "Hey, I know you might think you're too young, but believe me—just the spunk in you could light a fire!"

She grinned back, "Don't you mean *spark*?"

"Awwww . . . you! Watch that quick wit! Now get out there and start warming up, Captain!"

Grace pulled her 5'8" frame as tall as she could and walked to the middle of the court. She heard whispers as she passed: "How old is she?

Can she even play at a varsity level? Her parents probably paid for her to get on the team. She's never played Junior Varsity before—she has no idea what she's in for." She tightened her resolve and began to stretch.

Chloe pulled away from the huddles and said loud enough for everyone in the gym to hear, "Coach, I'm not playing under a ninth-grade captain. I'm a senior and have played for three years and worked hard to stand out. I'm not going to stay, and I'm sure others aren't either." She gave a defiant toss of her ponytail and snapped her head in Grace's direction. "If she leads, I'm out!"

The coach knew she would be the first to voice a complaint. "Chloe, I understand your concerns. It's a big move, but Grace brings experience and has great leadership ability. I'm not changing my mind." Chloe put her hands on her hips and marched out of the gym.

She was a good player but lacked character and wasn't committed to being a team player. She needed to lead the game herself or stand out with a fresh, risky move. The basics bored her, and the only consistency she had was pushing for a new direction.

Grace tried to focus on preparing for practice, but her mind raced in circles. *If only she had known! I'm not a good leader. At least I don't think I am. Am I, God? She wouldn't have left if she knew I was used to leading people younger than me, not older. I'm only 14. I don't know half the stuff they do! They could probably give a physics formula for serving a ball. I don't know anything but the fundamentals my dad drilled into my head! Pass-set-spike!* She watched as two more girls walked out. *God! What is happening? I'm not ready to lead—not like this!* She began to feel sick.

The team went from 12 to nine girls in less than 30 minutes. Grace's stomach started to churn and she asked to be excused. Once in the bathroom, she whispered her prayers out loud, "Lord, help me do this, because I don't know what to do. I need to talk to someone—like someone with skin. No offense."

She remembered her church youth leader and continued her conversation. "Hey God, Marissa was an All-American volleyball player in college! I've picked her brain for ways I could improve my game, but I bet she could help me lead too!" The churning stopped, and

Gracie was relieved. She had a plan. She already had a good relationship Marissa because they both loved volleyball. She was counting the days until youth group when she heard a whistle sound. It was time to hit the court.

She joined the girls and noticed they ran the warm-up drills slow, some even walked instead of doing sprints. She gave it her all. She was taught by her parents to always give her best, no matter what you're doing. The team ran around the indoor track, and most of them were out of breath by the second lap. Spiking? They missed time and again. Serving? They barely got the ball over the net.

Grace groaned. She was in awe, but not in a good way. The weight of the world landed squarely on her shoulders. *How am I going to help turn this around? Do I have to motivate them—in six weeks? HOW? These Field High "Tigers" are not just tame, they're lame!* She couldn't lighten her mood with her own humor and felt optimism sink out of reach. *I need to talk with Marissa—fast!*

That night, after Grace swept in to the house and gobbled down her supper, she called Marissa. "Oh. My. Goodness. Marissa? It's Grace. I have a huge problem, and I need your help!"

Marissa laughed, "I'm glad to help, if I can." Teenagers always had a healthy supply of drama, but she especially liked Grace. It was more than just a volleyball connection. She had a good head on her shoulders. "What's up?"

Gracie started in, "Well, for starters, I was named the new captain of the varsity volleyball team—"

Marissa cut in, "Cool! I knew you could—"

"No, Marissa! A bad team!" She poured out the details in a stream. "I'm so stressed out! First, it was embarrassing. The coach said if we don't win this year, the school is cutting the program, which is horrible. Then she said the team needed me. ME! A ninth grader! Like—how am I going to lead? I've never even hung out with kids older than me! One of the seniors stormed out and two of her friends quit on the spot—all because of me. Now there's only nine girls left, and I have no clue how to get them to trust me or even like me. We have six weeks to improve or we'll get slaughtered this season by mediocre teams! Can you help?"

Marissa listened and started in with empathy, "I'm so sorry, Gracie. Believe it or not, I've been there! Well, not leading people older than me, but I was on the other side. In high school, I played volleyball because it was something to do. I never gave it much thought. I just wanted to be a part of the team, and it did not matter to me if we won or lost."

Grace whispered, "No! Not you?"

"Yeah, me! At least until I had a captain that saw potential in me and changed my perspective. She believed in me, and it was a game changer! I know you can do the same. I actually use the same principles today that my team captain back in high school! Do you have something to write with?" She waited for Grace to get a pen and paper before she continued, "Here's what you need to do, and believe me, it works!"

Grace wrote down everything Marissa shared, but put big stars around the first one at the top of the page: #1: BELIEVE IN THEM! When Marissa finished, she paused and said, "Grace? Know this. I believe in you. You *can* do this."

"Wow, I needed to hear those words. I've always been determined to succeed, but this threw me for a loop! I want to be a good leader. I enjoy volleyball so much! I just wanted others around me to enjoy it too."

"Believe me, I understand!" Marissa encouraged Grace to take action right away. "You got this, girl!"

The next day, Grace brought Gatorade for all the girls and arrived early to start practicing the drills. She wanted to set the standard. She was committed to winning and hoped they would follow her example or at least catch a glimmer of it——a winner's attitude.

"We can do this, guys!" She continued to show up and play full out. She wasn't trying to show off—just show up the way she had been taught. She brought Gatorade without saying a word or asking anyone to chip in. She used it as an opportunity to gather around the cooler and ask questions. What's your favorite food? Who do you admire? What do you enjoy most about volleyball?

The walls came down as she got to know her teammates. It was tough at first and didn't come naturally, but Marissa believed in her, and each small success encouraged her to take another step outside of her comfort zone. Before long it didn't matter if she was "too young." She was capable.

By the fourth week, Grace posted notes over the locker room.

WE ARE WINNERS!
WE OVERCOME ADVERSITY TOGETHER!
WE ARE MORE THAN CONQUERERS!

Their spikes and serves improved along with their confidence. Grace celebrated them. The girls began to stay later at practice to get better. Grace stayed with them. If one girl didn't think she could run another lap, Grace ran beside her and encouraged her, "You can do this! I believe in you!"

Coach Tillman built upon the fundamentals. Grace built a solid core of confidence and community. The team finally trusted and believed in one another. It was good ground for the season. They gained momentum together and achieved much more than anyone imagined. When the finals were over, they didn't quite land on top, but their comeback saved the volleyball program.

How Can You Sparkle With Leadership?

I Believe in You

Grace's big #1 decision to believe in others helped her to make the decision to lead, but it wasn't easy. She had to step outside of her comfort zone with kindness and compassion and believe in others even when they didn't trust her yet. You can lead with the same actions and much more.

Has someone ever told you they believe in you? If not, I want you to know that I believe you can be a great leader! Maybe you already have the opportunity to step into a new leadership role or be a part of a team. Whether in basketball, volleyball, tennis, soccer, debate team, student newspaper, or student council, it's time to sparkle in your role!

There was a young man in the Bible named Timothy who was inexperienced and had a role to lead people who were far older than he was. We see his story through the letters of a strong leader who was writing to encourage and teach him. His commission was to lead with his character, not with his title. This is the most important and influential way you will lead and influence others: with who you are.

If you read First and Second Timothy in the Bible, you will find much encouragement as a young leader! Here are four traits Timothy's mentor shared with him. Each reflects a facet of admirable ways you can use to learn to lead well for the rest of your life.

Did I Just Say That?

1) *What you speak and say to others is important.* The Bible says, *"The tongue has the power of life and death, and those who love it will eat its fruit"* (Prov. 18: 21 NIV). Positive, affirming words give life to others. It gives them hope when they feel discouraged and comfort when they feel hurt. It can also allow you to celebrate someone else's win. Choose to speak words that build people up instead of tearing them down. Be generous with kind words and give others confidence. Remind them often: "I believe in you!"

Live It Out Loud

2) *How you live is also important.* God sees you as a *"capable, intelligent, and virtuous woman,"* (Prov. 31:10 AMPC). A virtuous

woman is a young lady whose path leads away from anything destructive. For example, you can be virtuous by avoiding gossip or staying busy and not being idle—hanging out in hallways during class or watching endless hours of television. You can choose to use your time to read a great book or practice a new skill. How about learning a new make-up application or trying a new hairstyle? Taking care of your appearance and reminding yourself that you're beautiful and valuable is powerful too! You are made to sparkle. Any time you invest in yourself, it will show up in your character. Others will see you shine! And through your confidence, they will see something different in you.

Enjoy Your Faith With Others

3) *Show others that you believe in a great God.* Romans 10:17 (CSB) says, *"So faith comes from what is heard, and what is heard comes through the message about Christ."* Every day, there are opportunities to reveal how good God is. He is the One who heals broken hearts. He brings peace in midst of challenging situations. God gives good counsel in the midst of confusion. By experiencing this, your life is a signpost for others! God wants you to share His goodness! Do you have a friend who needs a kind word to know she's not alone? Does your sibling need to know God's love or be reminded of His good plans? Is there a peer on social media who recently shared a difficult situation and needs your prayers? Have gently-used clothes? Donate to a friend in need or a homeless shelter. These are just a few ways you can share your precious faith.

Make a Radical Commitment

4) *Guard your heart.* Every day, you must decide to protect your heart or leave it vulnerable. Impure messages constantly bombard us through television, newspapers, social media, books, magazines, and music. The list goes on! Sexual thoughts can be sparked with something as simple as a commercial. It's a daily choice to be pure. God's grace and strength is stronger than anything in this world that can try to pull your heart away from Christ or His standard of purity.

When it comes to your body and sexuality, I encourage you to choose to save yourself for marriage. God will absolutely love this (and your parents will too)! Romans 12:1 (NIV) invites us to, *"to offer your bodies as a living sacrifice, holy and pleasing to God—this is your true and proper worship."* When you choose to save yourself for marriage, it's a great commitment with wonderful rewards. Even if you have compromised in this area, God is your healer. He loves you right where you are and can help you become strong and remain pure.

Choose today to walk a pure path. Guard your heart and avoid impure speech or conduct. Honor God with your precious body because you are valuable!

Sparkle & Shine

Reflect on what you've read!

Choose One Area: Write down the area you will begin to demonstrate these incredible leadership qualities. Don't be discouraged if you mess up or make a mistake, just get back up and continue on. You can do this! *"In the same way, let your light shine before others, so that* *they may see your good works and give glory to your Father who is in heaven"* (Matt. 5:16 NIV).

Write a Prayer: Now write a personal prayer to God seeking his wisdom and counsel to lead with confidence. *"God has not given us a spirit of fear, but of power and of love and of a sound mind"* (2 Tim. 1:7 NIV).

_____

_____

_____

_____

_____

_____

_____

_____

_____

_____

_____

"You are to lead by a different model.
If you want to be the greatest one, then live as
one called to serve others."

—MARK 10:43 (TPT)

CHAPTER THREE

Violet's Story
Sparkle With Courage

Violet's mother had a dream. She wanted her daughter to escape poverty. She stood with her hands on her hips in the middle of the kitchen as Violet dashed through on her way to a chess tournament. "Playing chess will not pay for college or get you a scholarship!"

Violet whirled around, "But mom, a win tonight will place me in regionals!" It was the biggest chess match in the school district, and winning would move her one step closer to a scholarship. She wanted to win with everything in her and show her mom that the uncanny gift for a game was worth something.

"It's a nice hobby, Violet, but it doesn't pay the bills." She noticed her daughter's shoulders droop and tried to explain, "We simply cannot afford to pay for your college. If you do not get a scholarship, then we cannot send you to college." She believed in Violet and wanted her to make something good out of her life, but playing chess for hours after school just didn't seem like the way to do it. "After tonight, you will put chess behind you and focus on your school work."

The direction was firm. Violet knew she couldn't argue—not now, at least. She wanted to stay sharp for the tournament. Mr. Blake, Valley High's chess coach, was counting on her.

At the end of her sophomore year, she played a game with some upperclassmen. A teacher walked by and noticed that she had a natural ability to solve problems and respond well under pressure. That teacher was Mr. Blake. He invited her to join the chess team.

She joined the next year, and Coach Blake took time to teach her the rules of the game. Everyone else on the team had played for years. She learned checkmate, castling, and how to move the king with confidence. She practiced every day after school and played against the top players. Over time her knack for chess turned into skill, and tonight she was ready to showcase her gift.

Violet stopped at the door, "I hope you come tonight!" She knew it could show her mother that she was gifted in many ways. She didn't wait for a response.

"I have to work," her mother said to the closed door.

The Valley High gymnasium buzzed with excitement. Violet watched as parents began to find seats in the bleachers—everyone except her mother. She closed her eyes and inhaled deeply. Disappointment threatened her confidence. She told herself, *I am smart! I am intelligent! I can do this!* But she still felt let down and wondered, *If I'm so gifted, why doesn't this matter to my mom? Why couldn't she come to the most important event of the year?* She scanned the crowd again. This time one familiar face appeared—her older brother. *At least someone believes in me*, she thought to herself.

Violet studied her competition as other teams gathered. They looked rich and self-assured, like they never lost anything to anyone— ever! She whispered, "Coach Blake, I can't do this." He looked at her quizzically as she continued, "Those other players are more qualified than I am. They attend better schools and have been playing chess for years. Years! And I haven't even played for one!"

He whispered back to her, "It's moments like these that define if fear will direct your choices—or courage. Choose courage, Violet. *You are a gifted* chess player!" She smiled, encouraged by his words.

There were 25 schools competing in their district and only the top eight students in each division would advance to the regional tournament. After that? State—with a chance to win college scholarships. The top winners also received cash prizes. Coach Blake told her she had a good shot at winning it all. She knew it was one way to show her mother that chess was valuable. She knew it wasn't a career path, but if it got her to college and opened up opportunities, surely her family would approve.

The gymnasium floor had long rows of tables and kids poured into place, two-by-two, ready to face off for their first round. Violet approached her table and waited for her opponent. She looked through the crowd one more time. *Mom? Is that . . . yes! You came!* She laughed at the stern look on her face. Violet didn't care. Her mom was there.

She bowed her head and breathed a silent prayer, *This is a great time to show my mom what I'm capable of, God. I NEED her to believe in me! I want her to see that this gift can be used for good, and I can really do something with it! Help me to make decisions from courage tonight. Thanks.*

A bright-eyed student swished into the seat across from Violet. "Praying? Am I that threatening?" She was one of those rich kids in designer clothes, but Violet liked her easy manner and warmth.

She joked back, "Oh no. I was praying FOR you!" They both laughed as the tournament director started the overview and game play rules. Violet was glad her mom was there to hear it and hoped she would be impressed. When he talked about advancement to the regional tournament, her heart jumped.

The two girls concentrated over each move. Their intensity got the attention of others as they finished their matches and waited for the next round. Eyes gravitated to their table as they maneuvered and slapped the clock.

Laughter bubbled out of her opponent as she blocked Violet's move. The room shushed her and she gave a flourish with her hand instead. Violet panicked! That was her signature move for a win! *What am I going to do?* She worried about what her mom would think if she lost the first round.

Breathe, girl, just breathe. She recalled Coach Blake's words: "Stay calm and use your mind to solve the problem before you. You're capable of solving problems." *That's right, she thought. I can solve problems.* She thought backward and forward through options and possibilities of each move. Time dissolved and more matches ended.

Finally, one option appeared that she hadn't considered before. It would take a series of moves, but she doubted her opponent would catch on in time. Violet made the move and the girl's eyes sparkled, but she whispered, "Are you sure?" It looked like she just handed her the game.

Violet nodded, "I'm sure."

"Well? Okay," she conceded and proceeded to roll out classic moves.

Violet grinned when her series put the final crunch on the surprise attack, "Checkmate!" The crowd stood and applauded, despite the rule that spectators must maintain silence. Even the tournament director clapped before quieting the crowd. Violet looked at the stands and saw her mother on her feet too—smiling!

Violet's heart soared through the next four rounds. She won each match. While score were tallied, she found her family. Her mom wrapped her in a hug and said, "Violet, I am proud of you. Chess isn't one of my favorite activities, but I believe you can do both—as long as you keep your academics first."

Violet brimmed with hope and confidence. She hugged her mom back—tight. "Thanks, Mom." She knew that God's plans for her are good, and now her mother saw value in it too.

Choose Courage

There will be people who do not understand your involvement in a school activity such as the debate team or choir. They may not think volunteering at a soup kitchen isn't worth your time. It can even be those closest to you who don't see the value in what is important to you. It can lead to conflicting thoughts within you, and you may wonder if it's worth the time and effort.

Here are some questions to help you decide if you should pursue the activity. "Does this activity hurt anyone?" "Does it help me become a better person or strengthen character qualities like patience, kindness, or gentleness?" Finally, "Does it keep me on track in my studies or move me toward a brighter future?" If you answered yes, then it sounds like this could be a God-given activity for you or a gifting to develop. Be sure to talk to God about it, He will give you peace about His plans.

Sometimes obeying God will not be easy. If there is someone who does not support your activities, prayerfully ask God to show them how this activity is beneficial. If it happens to be your parents, understand that they mean well and their concern is often because they want the best for you, then ask God to show them the truth. He can reveal how it truly is a blessing to you!

How Can You Sparkle With Courage?

Someone Believes in You

You may feel lonely when you are pursuing something others don't understand. It may feel like there is no one who believes in you. But if there is just one person who does, it makes a huge difference! You may even be scared to stand up for something you believe when it goes against society.

Esther was a young woman in the Bible who came out of obscurity and became a queen. Her uncle raised her with godly beliefs, and even though her parents died, she had a firm foundation in her Jewish faith. One day, a decree was passed to kill all of the Jews in the land. Esther's uncle pleaded with her to save the lives of Jewish people and bring the matter before the king. But no one was allowed to see the king without an invitation, not even the queen. It was grounds for death!

She was afraid, but her uncle believed she could do it. He encouraged her with these words: *"And who knows but that you have come to your royal position for such a time as this*?" (Esther 4:14 NIV). Esther risked her life and went before the king. He showed mercy and

51

granted her wish. God gave her an idea to invite the king and the man who made the decree to a dinner and share her request there. When the king realized what had been done, he was angry! Everything turned around in a moment, and she was able to save her people.

It wasn't easy for Esther. She had to make the choice to put herself on the line for what was right, even though the risk to her was great. God had a purpose for her to fulfill, and her uncle is the one who encouraged her to do it. She faced fear, chose to intervene, and rescued others.

God gives us gifts and talents and when he does, he uses it for a good purpose. Esther may have wondered if God could really use her. We don't know about other gifts and talents, but she was beautiful. The king chose her out of all the young women in the land. From that one simple attribute, God was able to bring her to a place of influence, and when the time came, she rose to the challenge. She was brave and used her influence for the good of others.

The gift you have inside you is a God given gift. Choose to cultivate it and set some goals for yourself. If you find yourself struggling, set small goals along the way. Taking one step in the right direction day-by-day will help you reach your goal. Esther may have done this as well. When she went before the king, she didn't tell him the reason why yet. She invited him to dinner instead. When he came and asked about her request, she didn't tell him—again—but invited him to a second dinner. Maybe she struggled? Maybe this was a way of taking small steps? We don't know because the Bible doesn't reveal that part. But I do know this, if you will take one small step in the right direction, God will meet you there and help you take the next one.

Setting goals also helps you be intentional with your time. Your goal will give you something to focus on. And when you can see the next steps and intentionally invest your time, you will achieve so much more than what you just wished and dreamed!

Choose to give God your "brave best," and you will continue to grow and shine!

Sparkle & Shine

Reflect on what you've read!

Make a Personal Inventory: What skills do you have? What are you passionate about? Do you have gifts that have gone unnoticed or dreams that you haven't shared with anyone? Write them down here!

Write a Prayer: Ask God to show you what He has placed in you and help you boldly go after the dreams in your heart.

_____

_____

_____

_____

_____

_____

_____

_____

_____

_____

Made to Sparkle

Be strong and very courageous. Be careful to
obey all the law my servant Moses gave you;
do not turn from it to the right or to the left,
that you may be successful wherever you go."

—JOSHUA 1:7 (NIV)

CHAPTER FOUR

Olivia's Story
Sparkle With Confidence

Olivia stepped to the podium, ready to give her graduation speech on hope. She excelled with a 4.0 grade point average and held a scholarship to the school of her dreams, but hidden behind her success was a battle with depression and hopelessness. Even though she was the class president, she fought against feeling unwanted and unloved.

Her struggle wasn't with school or peers. All year long, as her future burned bright before her, it reminded her of her mother's loss—and hers too. She never knew her grandparents or her father. She was raised by a single mother who refused to abort her. It caused a rift in the family because her mom's parents thought it "ruined" their dreams for their daughter to be successful in life—the success Olivia felt like she was stepping into instead of her mom.

She stood before her classmates, friends, and family with an ache in her heart. In all of her 18 years, she never seen or known any family other than her mother. Hope was her theme because it pulled her through the darkest moments of her life. She almost gave up when she felt others had given up on her, but that night she stood before them as a story yet to be heard: All Things Are Possible.

Olivia's mother waved from the crowd. The broad, beautiful smile she had known all her life fueled her resolve to share her vulnerable moments. She was about to tell 800 seniors, one of the largest schools in the city, about how she felt insecure and unsure of herself despite academic honors, sports, and activities that earned her accolades. She wanted them to know: "You are valuable, even if you don't know your father or mother. You matter to the One in Heaven."

Her journey was a long process. She knew what it was like to be beautiful on the outside but empty on the inside. Ultimately God filled the void, but until she knew His love, it felt like she hauled a backpack filled with bricks. Instead of hurting her back, her heart ached—badly! Thoughts plagued her, especially the last year of high school. *Why didn't my daddy ever try to find me? How come my grandparents didn't call for the holidays?* Her mother called them every year, but no one ever answered or returned a call. *Didn't they love her? Didn't they love me?* Olivia's value and self-worth diminished with each aching question and thought. She felt like an accident.

Several months earlier, Olivia opened up and voiced her concerns to her mother. Her mom hugged her in a tight embrace, and they cried together. Then she grabbed her Bible and opened it. The pages were worn with scriptures highlighted yellow, light blue, and green. Her faith brought her through much as a single mother. She began to show Olivia what God, the Creator of the universe, thought of her.

Her tender voice spoke truth, "Olivia, God says you're fearfully and wonderfully made. He says He is a father to the fatherless, and you are His masterpiece." Olivia wanted to believe every part of it, but her heart still felt heavy. Her mother's words couldn't immediately wipe away the pain that filled her heart or the tears that filled her eyes.

For years, Olivia tried to hide pain through academics and activities, but the weight of it all began to get to her. Kids talked about their fathers and families every day. They spent time together. Even kids who had broken homes still saw their dad and went out to eat or watched movies together. She watched as her friend's grandparents attend award ceremonies and performances. Every conversation and event was a painful reminder to Olivia that her family was incomplete. She felt deeply wounded and needed healing. She needed hope!

Olivia decided to take the scriptures her mom shared and read them again for herself. She didn't want unanswered questions or hurt to cause her to give up and not care about life. As she began to trust God, her mother's voice constantly reminded her: "You have a bright future before you, Olivia. God sees you as special!" She just had to believe it.

It wasn't instant, but over the remaining weeks and months of the school year, God's Word began to strengthen her. At first it seemed far away, but as she continued to focus on what God said about her and resist the feelings of inferiority, her confidence grew as hope came alive.

That night at graduation, Olivia knew God wanted her to share hope with her classmates. She knew her mother was proud of her, but she was proud of her mother too. Emotion flooded her with the realization that she fought for Olivia and sacrificed her family for what she felt was right. It was tough, but she did succeed after all! She raised a smart daughter.

She opened her speech and set the papers on the podium. Before beginning, she looked at her mother's face in the crowd. She wanted to continue to make her proud. "Mom, this is for you." Two older people sat next to her mother, and one leaned in to whisper something—they all smiled. Their faces looked familiar! Suddenly Olivia remembered a photo her mother had on the fireplace shelf. It was her grandparents!

Mixed emotions flooded in—anger, sadness, joy, wonder. Thoughts flashed while she hesitated. *Why did they take so long?* But happiness settled quickly. They came for one of the important moments of her life!

She knew then that her message was not just for her classmates, it was for her grandparents. They would also see the God who made the difference in her life and helped her become the young woman who stood before them that night.

Olivia's voice was strong and compassionate as it washed over the crowd. "I used to think I was an accident." She paused and looked at the faces. Some showed surprise. "But I was rescued by hope." Her story unfolded from her heart. Tears came to some as their hearts opened. She showed them how God was her hope in darkness and concluded with, "Now I know that I am special. I am created for a purpose. God has plans for my life, and He has plans for yours too."

How Can You Sparkle With Confidence?

God Sees Something in You

Have you ever felt like Olivia, feeling as though you were an accident? Forgotten? Unloved? Even if you feel overlooked by the world around you, God knows you by name. Many scriptures say "I know you by name" or "I have called you by your name." Jesus said, *"I am the good shepherd; I know my own sheep, and they know me"* (John 10:14 NIV).

God sees something special in you. You are beautiful, gorgeous, and "fearfully and wonderfully made" (PS. 139:14 KJV). Wait, He says more! Think about your beautiful hair for a second. In His Incredible Book, God says, *"And the very hairs on your head are all numbered. So don't be afraid; you are more valuable to God than a whole flock of sparrows"* (Luke 12:7 NIV). He knows the number of hairs on your head. God values *you*!

It gets even better because God does not stop there. The Bible is filled with so many wonderful promises of how wonderful you are. *"How precious are your thoughts about me, O God. They cannot be numbered! I can't even count them; they outnumber the grains of sand! And when I wake up, you are still with me!"* (Psalm 139:17–18 NLT).

Circumstances try to define who we are and convince us that our worth is found in what we can accomplish or who others think we are. But true self-worth that is based upon God's truth gives us a strong foundation. Why? Because He never changes. *"Jesus Christ is the same yesterday and forever"* (Hebrews 13:8 NIV).

Accepting these truths can be difficult at first. I encourage you to write down these scriptures and begin to study them or read them daily. This will help replace wrong thoughts or negative thoughts that comes to your mind about who you really are. You are made to sparkle with confidence. As you think on God's amazing words, I pray confidence builds in your heart. You will be strengthened and encouraged to know You truly are fearfully and wonderful made. You are created for a purpose.

Sparkle & Shine

Reflect on what you've read!

Challenge: Start your day with 10 minutes to read the Bible. When you plan God's Word in your heart like a seed and water it consistently, it will grow and flourish! Begin with Psalm 139. Read the entire chapter and highlight or write down the scripture that stands out to you. You will begin to see you truly are a treasure! Write one of your favorite portions here:

Did you grow up without a father? Maybe your parents are not involved in your life. It could be that one or both died while you were young. Perhaps you lost someone close to you. Use the following scriptures to find encouragement and strength.

> To the fatherless he is a father.
> To the widow he is a champion friend.
> To the lonely he makes them part of a family.

—PSALM 68:5—6 (TPT)

When my father and my mother forsake me,
then the Lord will take me up.

—PSALM 27:10 (KJV)

The Lord is near to the brokenhearted
and saves the crushed in spirit.

—PSALM 34:18 (ESV)

Write a Prayer: You can heal from loss. Write down a prayer asking God to help you heal from wounds from a loved one not being in your life. His deep love for you holds strength and wisdom. It will take time, but take a step forward every day toward hope. You can still sparkle and overcome any hurts you face!

_____

_____

_____

_____

_____

_____

_____

_____

_____

_____

_____

_____

PS. I would love to pray for you! Contact me at lanieryv@gmail.com. I have personally experienced healing from the hurts of loved ones not being in my life (see the epilogue for a glimpse of my story). It is possible to sparkle and shine after loss!

Jasmine's Story
Sparkle With Clear Vision

Algebra II was just like every other math class Jasmine had taken—awful. She couldn't stand numbers. Whenever the teacher explained equations, she drifted off in daydreams of becoming a surgeon. But Jasmine had a problem. Top colleges for her dream career also demanded top grades, and she was failing.

Yet she was sure that God had placed that dream in her heart. Jasmine promised her aunt that she would do something remarkable with her life. After her aunt suffered through cancer and passed away, her dream became an insatiable desire. All she could think about was rising in the ranks as the next great surgeon to treat cancer patients and help people live longer.

But desire fizzled when it came to Algebra. Somehow she cruised through other math courses and made it work . . . barely. This was different. She simply couldn't understand it and couldn't stand the thought of putting forth that kind of energy again.

Jasmine really wanted to honor her word to her aunt. She researched the top schools for surgeons, and the only way for her to have a shot at those colleges was to step up her game. She knew in her heart she needed to do better, but couldn't make herself stop laughing, joking, and passing notes with friends during class. At times, she distracted herself with her cell phone—scrolling through posts and photos, looking for the latest, greatest, funniest status.

A big exam was around the corner, and Jasmine didn't want to think about it. She tried tutoring. It didn't help. She tried studying extra hard before other tests and still failed. She didn't know what to do, but she knew things had to change. Her grade in this class was crucial! Not only would her grade point average help her get accepted, it might qualify her for a scholarship!

The possibility of missing out on her dream weighed heavy. Perhaps she could settle on a lesser-known college with a mediocre program? Her heart fell at the thought of anything less. She silently wondered,

"God, why did You put this dream in my heart without putting math in my mind?"

Jasmine didn't really expect God to answer, but a thought came instead, "I should ask my mom what to do."

Her mother advised her to talk with her math teacher and seek his counsel too. "See how he can help you in this situation. Perhaps he has some other solutions?"

Mr. Adrian was a popular teacher. Even though he taught Jasmine's least favorite subjects, she liked him. He had a great personality and was always eager to help his students. When they came to class, he always encouraged them by name. "Good morning, Alex! So glad you're here today!" "How's tennis, Emma?" "How are you doing today, Jasmine?"

After class, she went to Mr. Adrian. "I'm failing and don't know what to do," she confessed. "I tried tutoring and extra studying, but nothing worked. I really want to get into a great college, and my top school requires me to have a B+ average in math to be considered. I feel like it's impossible!"

Mr. Arian sympathized with her. "You know, when I was in high school, I was the same way."

"Wait. What?" Jasmine couldn't imagine it. "Really?"

He laughed, "Yes, really! I had a hard time with math."

Jasmine raised her eyebrow and gave him a disbelieving look.

Mr. Adrian continued, "I didn't like it at all. Math just wasn't my thing. But one day, a community leader and mentor of mine said, 'If you want to be successful at anything, you must have focus. Discipline yourself. Study daily. Make it a priority. Focus and you'll reach your goals.' I took his advice seriously because I wanted to be successful—especially as an engineer."

Jasmine saw his point, but wondered about his dream. "But you're not an engineer. What happened?"

A broad smile crossed his face, "*This* happened—a moment just like this! Someone gave me great advice, and I began to apply myself. Turns out, math was pretty great once I understood it! I got into the school I wanted and began my studies as an engineer, but I couldn't get away from the power of making a difference. I switched my major and decided to become a teacher so I could help students right where they are—in school."

Jasmine smiled back at him. "Thanks, Mr. Adrian. I think I know what I need to do!" Her answer wasn't in last-ditch efforts and other people tutoring her; it was right there in class and in the choices she made with her free time.

The next day, she turned her cell phone off and left it in her purse. She paid attention as Mr. Adrian taught. Instead of chatting with friends until it was time to go to bed, she studied every day instead of cramming for a test. She had a dream to make a difference too.

Friends wondered what happened and pressured her for their usual hang out time, but Jasmine was determined. It was more than getting a good grade; she wanted to do good in the world and knew she needed to change to make it happen. Every other class started to shine too—especially science. It was easy to breeze through and get decent grades in subjects she liked, but her new focus helped her skyrocket to the top of her class!

She was choosing things for her future now. She still spent time with her friends on weekends, but instead of hanging out after school studying boys, fashion, and the latest gossip, she decided to study math and science.

Jasmine picked up new ideas to help her focus. She wrote down the big vision for her life, but she also wrote down a goal for each class. It was simple—just one sentence about what she wanted to achieve in each one. The more she focused, the more she accomplished!

By the time graduation arrived, the hard work and effort paid off. Her new B+ average got her in the door at the college of her dreams, and her new focused mindset earned a scholarship towards tuition. The clear vision she created paved the way for an education and career that would have made Jasmine's aunt proud!

How To Sparkle With Vision

Priorities, Priorities, Priorities

Discipline. *Ugh*! Who loves that word? I honestly don't think anyone does at first. On the surface it sounds boring and unexciting. "I'm missing out on all the fun!" It seems mundane and repetitive. "You mean I have to do this again? Like, tomorrow?"

But what if you looked deeper? Ah! Yes, discipline combined with passion or purpose is exciting! If that sounds crazy to you, just imagine what it would look like on the other side. Instead of wishing, you're actually living your dream!

What does that mean now? Choices. Priorities.

When you choose to practice or study something daily until you become well developed in that area, you can now master it. In other words, it's great! It also means that you are choosing to say no to something else, so you can say yes to a better and brighter future. You're working towards a great "A+" in a class, instead of settling for a C or letting it all slide by with an F.

There was someone in the Bible who had a routine and purpose combined—Jesus. Even as a child, the soles of his shoes traveled the path to the temple instead of following other paths. He was already God's Son, yet His desire to grow in His Father's ways created priorities, and He spent time listening. He listened as leaders shared passionately about God's laws and commands. His little heart could have burst with joy, for He was on a good path!

He prepared His heart for what He was born for—to bring salvation, forgiveness of sins, and a new relationship with God to people. Jesus had a desire to do something great with His life, and you can too!

You Hold the Power of Focus

Did you know God has good paths for your life? Jeremiah 29:11 (NLT) says, *"'For I know the plans I have for you'" says the Lord. 'They are plans for good and not for disaster, to give you a future and a hope.'"*

Where should you start? For Him, it started with studying. May I encourage you to become passionate about your studies? Whether you desire to become a scientist, teacher, lawyer, doctor, senator, or fashion designer, there are endless books in the library or online that you can access and begin to read about your profession. Read about people who achieved great success in your career. Be curious!

Why is knowledge important? God says that without knowledge we perish or we're not successful in life (Hosea 4:6). Besides, knowledge opens up doors for us that no one can shut. Success is not an accident. We must do things intentionally—just like Jesus. Jesus was so intentional about what He wanted to do. He wanted to know His Father and do good. He was passionate about doing the right thing, and He chose to take time to sit before teachers who could help Him.

There is no better way to achieve success than to seek out mentors, people who have walked the path before you. You can call them your "north stars" as they will point you in the direction you should go. Seek teachers who believe in you—those who always encourage you, the teachers who often ask, "How is your day going?"

Jesus sat with teachers because He knew they had information He needed to help Him succeed. He knew it made a great difference.

Can you take the next step to evaluate? Find teachers that really want to invest in your life and see you reach your potential. You will achieve your dreams!

Sparkle & Shine

Reflect on what you've read!

What are your dreams? Write down your desires in the space below. God says, *"Delight yourself in the Lord, and he will give you the desires of your heart"* (Ps. 37:4 NIV). He also says, *"Write the vision; make it plain on tablets, so he may run who reads it"* (Hab. 2:2 NIV).

Be Curious: Find a book on your desired field. Write down some options here. Stir your curiosity and discover what it takes to get to where you want to go. I believe you will get there and be great!

A focused mindset is possible! Remember: There will be many distractions—social media, idly chatting on the phone, gossiping, and watching endless TV shows. Make a decision to be all-in like Jesus with your future. God's plans for your life are really good! Choose to spend your time wisely when it comes to friends and social media.

Both are good, but keep your priorities before you. Make a list. What is important to you? Where do you want to go?

What are your priorities?

> "After three days they found Jesus in the temple courts, sitting among the teachers, listening to them and asking them questions."
>
> —LUKE 2:46 (NIV)

Epilogue

Imagine ... a phone call informs a 19-year-old college sophomore that her father was found dead on the floor of his apartment.

This rocked my world in 2005. My dad had a heart attack and suddenly left my world.

Imagine four years later ... a phone call informs the young college graduate, who is pursuing her dream career in another city away from home, that her mother has two weeks to live.

This rocked my world again. My mother had stage-four cancer but told no one. Both of my parents passed away by the time I was 25 years old. I know the hurt, pain, and confusion of loss. I also know the power of faith.

When we draw near to God with our deepest hurts or loss, He brings healing. I can tell you firsthand that He brings hope and encouragement. It can come in many ways. Sometimes God brings friends to lift you up. Other times, He inspires a sermon to encourage you. Even if it is just you and God, he can surround you with love.

My friend, if you have gone through a loss, please allow God to be your rock through the situation. He will bring strength and peace through His Word and the people around you. Whether it is a counselor, mentor, pastor, dear relative, or trusted friend, be open to tell someone around you who can pray for you too. I received counseling when my dad passed away, and it helped me. Talking with others about your hurts can bring healing and help you see that there is still a future for you.

I would love to pray for you.

Contact me at lanieryv@gmail.com.

Made to Sparkle

Made to Sparkle

Made to Sparkle

CPSIA information can be obtained
at www.ICGtesting.com
Printed in the USA
BVHW030108300421
606131BV00008B/827

9 780578 884905